Teaching Healthy Cooking and Nutrition

in Primary Schools, Book 3

Cheesy Biscuits, Potato Salad, Apple Muffins and Other Recipes

Sandra Mulvany

Brilliant
PUBLICATIONS

We hope you and your pupils enjoy trying out the recipes in this book and learning about healthy eating. Brilliant Publications publishes many other books to help primary school teachers. To find out more details on all of our titles, including those listed below, please log onto our website: www.brilliantpublications.co.uk.

Other titles in the Teaching Healthy Cooking and Nutrition in Primary Schools series:

Other titles published by Brilliant Publications

Published by Brilliant Publications
Unit 10,
Sparrow Hall Farm,
Edlesborough,
Dunstable,
Bedfordshire,
LU6 2ES

www.brilliantpublications.co.uk

The name Brilliant Publications
and the logo are registered trade marks.

Written by Sandra Mulvany
Illustrated by Kerry Ingham
Cover design by Brilliant Publications
Photography by Brilliant Publications
Printed in the UK

© 2008 Sandra Mulvany (text); Brilliant Publications
(photography, design and layout)

Printed ISBN 978-1-78317-110-1
e-book ISBN 978-1-78317-116-3

The first edition of this book, published in 2008, had the
title: Healthy Cooking for Primary Schools, Book 3.
This second edition was first printed and published in
the UK in 2014

10 9 8 7 6 5 4 3 2 1

Contents

Contents (cont.)

Introduction and Links to the National Curriculum

The *Teaching Healthy Cooking and Nutrition in Primary Schools* series is a practical school programme for schools. It focuses on the progression in cooking skills through easy-to-follow recipes. Essential cooking skills, theory and health and safety points are introduced progressively throughout the series.

The programme is designed to teach pupils practical cooking whilst incorporating the theory into the hands-on activity. Each of the five books in the series contains 12 recipes, together with visual lesson structure cards, visual learning objectives and photographs of the food – all of which are photocopiable.

All the recipes are presented in two formats, one laid out in a traditional way and one in a visual step-by-step format, enabling the recipes to be used with pupils of all ages or with groups with differing reading abilities. It is recommended that, after a cooking session, the recipes are photocopied and sent home with pupils, so that children can try making the recipes at home.

There are two assessment sheets in the book (on pages 85–86). The assessment sheets test and reinforce the practical and theoretical knowledge gained. You will also find a photocopiable certificate on page 87 for when pupils have completed all the tasks.

This second edition of *Teaching Healthy Cooking and Nutrition in Primary Schools* has been amended to ensure that it addresses the requirements of the National Curriculum for England (September 2014). The programmes of study state that pupils should be taught how to cook and apply the principles of nutrition and healthy eating. It aims to instil in pupils a love of cooking and to teach them a life skill that will enable pupils to feed themselves and others affordably and well, now and in later life.

Key Stage 1 pupils should be taught to use the basic principles of a healthy and varied diet to prepare dishes and understand where food comes from.

Key Stage 2 pupils should be taught to:
* understand and apply the principles of a healthy and varied diet
* prepare and cook a variety of predominantly savoury dishes using a range of cooking techniques
* understand seasonality, and know where and how a variety of ingredients are grown, reared, caught and processed.

The series also links well with the Health and Wellbeing section of the Scottish Curriculum for Excellence and the Guidance on the Schools (Health Promotion and Nutrition) (Scotland) Act 2007.

How to Use the Resources

All ingredients are based on two pupils sharing, and the timings will all fit into a double lesson of approximately 80 minutes. We recommend you use low-fat options where possible.

Make a display using the Visual Lesson Structure Cards (pages 7–10) and pictures of the recipe and skill to be focussed on in the lesson (colour versions of the photographs can be downloaded from the Brilliant Publications' website).

Keep the skill, theory and health and safety point sheets to hand so that you can refer to them when demonstrating to pupils. (The language has been kept as simple as possible on these sheets, so you may wish to give copies to your pupils as well.)

Choose the best format of the recipe to use for each pair of children and photocopy sufficient copies. The illustrated versions of the recipes can be photocopied onto either an A3 sheet (if space is an issue, fold it in half so that you view six steps at a time), or reduced to A4 size.

If you place the recipes and other sheets in clear plastic wallets (or laminate them), they can be used again and again.

Encourage children to gather together all the ingredients and equipment they need before starting. They could tick things off on their copy of the recipe.

Demonstrate the recipe 2–3 steps at a time, introducing the skill, theory and health and safety points as you progress through the recipe.

An important aspect of learning to cook is learning to work together. You may wish to display the Discussion cards on pages 11–12 (Communicate, Share, Help, Be pleasant) so that you can refer to these throughout the lesson.

The assessment sheets on pages 85 and 86 provide a fun way of testing the practical and theoretical knowledge gained. The Certificate of Achievement on page 87 can either be used as an ongoing record or be given out when all the recipes in the book have been completed.

On pages 88–89 there is a chart giving some suggestions for adapting the recipes for children with allergies and intolerances, and/or religious and lifestyle considerations. None of the recipes use nuts. Before you start any cooking activities, you should send home a letter asking parents to inform you if there are any allergy/lifestyle/religious considerations that you need to take into account. You may need to follow this up with a letter or phone call to clarify any issues raised. A useful chart listing some religious food customs can be found at: www.childrensfoodtrust.org.uk/assets/the-standards/3food-customs.pdf.

Above all, have fun and enjoy cooking!

Today We are Making

1

Today We are Learning

2

Read Recipe

3

Wash Hands and Prepare

4

Cook

5

Clear Away

6

Tasting

7

We Have Learnt

8

Communicate

It is vital to have good communication in a cooking environment. If you are working with a partner, it is important to say what you are doing and to agree on who does what. You have to talk about what you would like to do and listen to what your partner wants to do. Then you have to work out a way to make it fair for both of you. You can only come to an agreement if you talk together!

You should also let others know if there are any dangers, such as you opening the oven or if water has been spilt on the floor. Talking is absolutely key to good cooking habits. The better you are at communicating, the better you are at cooking in a school environment.

Share

Good sharing follows on from good communicating. If you have communicated well, you will have reached a fair decision about sharing. Sharing works best when it has been done fairly and everyone is happy. Sharing is particularly difficult if it involves doing something really exciting or really boring. You have to imagine that the other person feels very much like yourself. This can be hard to imagine, but it is an important lesson to learn. Sharing is a lot easier when you talk together about things.

Help

It is important to be able to help others, but it is also important to accept help from others. Help is a two-way thing. If you are offering your help to someone else, it is important that you choose your words carefully. Be kind in giving your help, as it can be hard to accept help given with harsh words. If you have communicated well, you will be able to help each other well. If you are very capable, offer your help kindly, but also let others help you in return, even if it is to do with something you feel you might already know about.

Be pleasant

It is, in fact, very simple to be pleasant. Look at and listen to the person you are working with and notice something he or she does well. Then say something pleasant about that. You will soon discover that the more pleasant you are to people, the more pleasant they are back to you. You can also do something pleasant, like smile at a person or pat someone kindly on the back. Don't just wait for someone to be pleasant to you; try to be the first one to say or do something pleasant.

Cheesy Biscuits

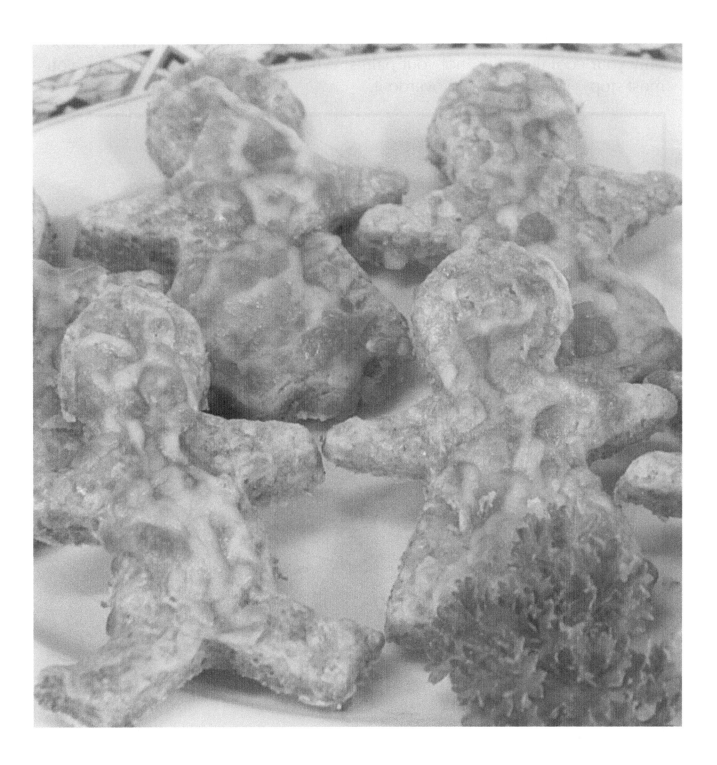

How to Rub in

It can be hard to rub margarine into flour. When you rub in, you first have to cover the margarine with flour and then gently lift the margarine as well as the flour. It is as much to do with the flour as it is to do with the margarine. Never just touch the margarine; always use all the flour to get to the margarine. Use only your cool fingertips, not your palms. When it looks like bread crumbs, you must stop – it is very easy to overdo it.

Food Changes When Heated

Cooking can improve the taste, smell and appearance of food. Moreover, food actually changes when you cook it. Starch grains swell and absorb liquid when boiled, like rice. The cellulose walls in fruit and vegetables break down and soften, as with boiled carrots. Liquid foods with protein in, such as eggs, change from a liquid state to a solid state when heated. This is called coagulation. Most minerals and some vitamins are water-soluble, so they leak into any water they are placed in. Where possible, re-use the cooking water, such as in gravy, so you really do get the most out of the food.

Be aware of what the cooking process does to your food.

Contamination from Coughing and Sneezing

Be very careful when coughing and sneezing. Coughs and sneezes can spread disease through the infectious droplets they produce. In one sneeze there can be as many as 40,000 droplets released at an approximate rate of 100mph. This is bad for other people as well as for any food you are preparing. Therefore, if you have to cough or sneeze, remove yourself from the food area, or turn away and cover your mouth and nose with your hands if you don't have a handkerchief at the ready. Always wash your hands thoroughly after having done this.

Cheesy Biscuits

Ingredients:
75g wholemeal flour   50g plain flour   75g margarine
Pinch of salt and pepper   75g cheese   2 egg yolks

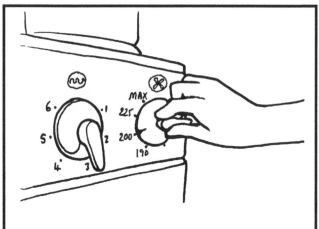

1. Put the oven on 200°C.

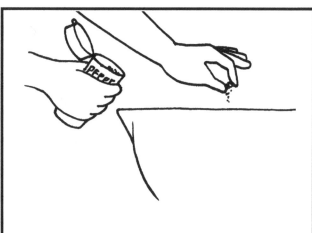

2. Mix the flours; rub in the margarine.

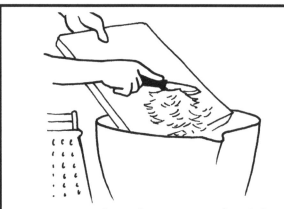

3. Add salt and pepper.

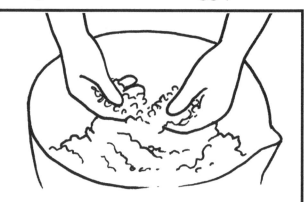

4. Separate the 2 egg yolks. Whisk and add to bowl.

5. Grate the cheese and add most to bowl.

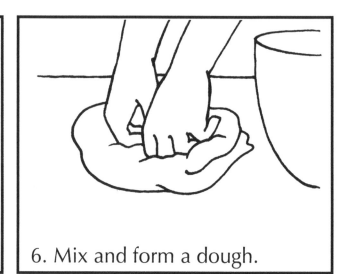

6. Mix and form a dough.

Cheesy Biscuits (cont.)

Recipe

Equipment:

Mixing bowl	Whisk/fork	Mixing spoon	Biscuit cutter
Brush	Baking tray	Egg cup	Small plate Scales Grater

7. Roll out the dough.

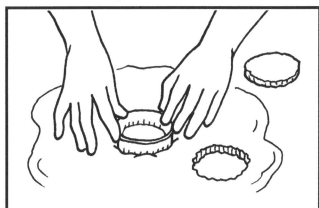

8. Use a biscuit cutter to cut the biscuits.

9. Put on a greased baking tray.

10. Brush the biscuits with egg.

11. Sprinkle with cheese.

12. Bake in oven for 10 minutes.

Recipe

Cheesy Biscuits

Ingredients:
75g wholemeal flour
50g plain flour
75g margarine
Pinch of salt and pepper
75g cheese
2 egg yolks

Equipment:
Mixing bowl
Whisk/fork
Mixing spoon
Biscuit cutter
Brush
Baking tray
Egg cup
Small plate
Scales
Grater

Instructions:

1. Put the oven on 200°C.

2. Mix the flours; rub in the margarine.

3. Add salt and pepper.

4. Separate the 2 egg yolks. Whisk and add to bowl.

5. Grate the cheese and add most to bowl.

6. Mix and form a dough.

7. Roll out the dough.

8. Use a biscuit cutter to cut the biscuits.

9. Put on a greased baking tray.

10. Brush the biscuits with egg.

11. Sprinkle with cheese.

12. Bake in oven for 10 minutes.

Potato Salad

How to Peel a Potato

It can be quite hard to peel a potato. It is also quite dangerous, as your fingers are very near the peeler. Watch a demonstration of a potato being peeled and observe how the thumb is used to press against the potato. However, remember that there are lots of vitamins in most peels of fruit and vegetables. Therefore, if possible, cook the vegetables with the peel on, particularly if the vegetable is still young and fresh. If you do have to peel it, try to peel it as thinly as possible.

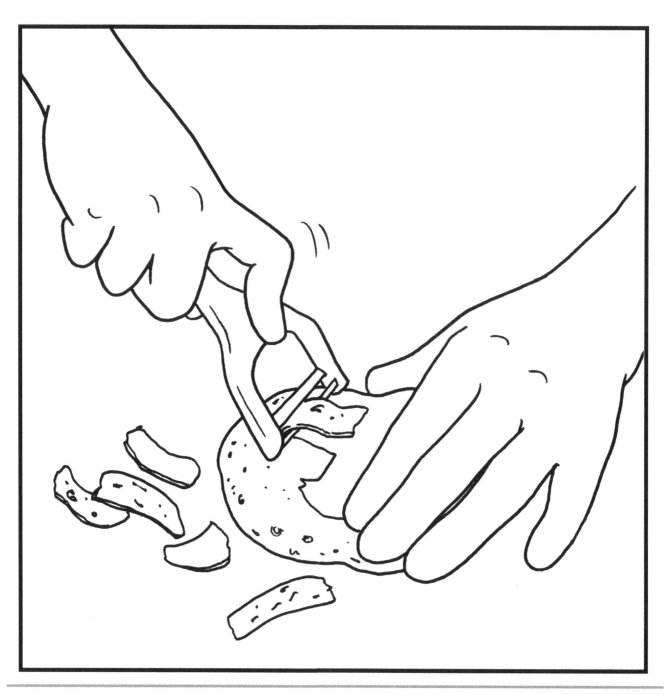

Vitamin C Dissolves in Water

Potatoes are full of carbohydrates, but they also contain a lot of vitamin C. Much of this is in and just under the skin, but there is also a lot of vitamin C in the potato itself. However, vitamin C dissolves in water. This means that, as soon as you submerge a potato in water, it begins to "leak" vitamin C into the water. The key, therefore, is to prepare the potato immediately prior to boiling it and if possible to use the vegetable water as gravy.

Reasons to Keep Knife Handles Clean

It is important to keep knife handles as clean and dry as possible. This is because a knife handle can become slippery and difficult to hold safely when it gets wet. If you lose your grip on a knife handle, you could end up cutting yourself.

Recipe

Potato Salad

Ingredients:

300g potatoes   3 rashers streaky bacon 1 onion Water
Pinch of pepper   4 tbsp mayonnaise   Fresh chives

1. Put water in a saucepan and put on hob.

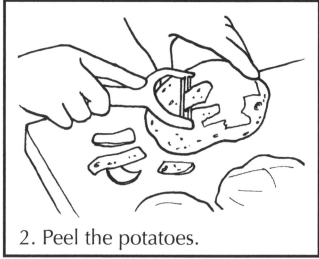

2. Peel the potatoes.

3. Cut potatoes and put in boiling water.

4. Cut bacon into small pieces.

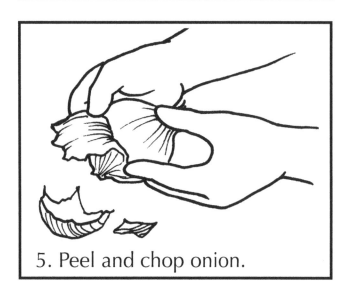

5. Peel and chop onion.

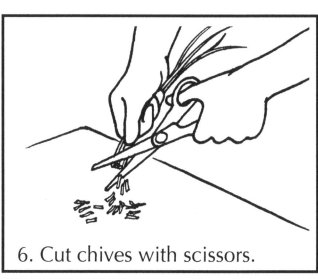

6. Cut chives with scissors.

Potato Salad

Recipe

Equipment:

Saucepan	Turner	Potato peeler	Colander
Sharp knife	Tablespoon	Chopping board	Mixing bowl
Scissors	Mixing spoon	Frying pan	Scales

7. Fry bacon in frying pan. Remove when cooked.

8. Fry onions in frying pan.

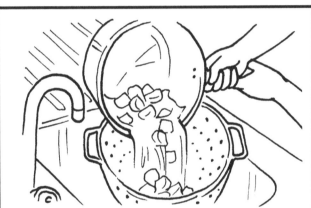

9. Drain potatoes when ready and put in bowl.

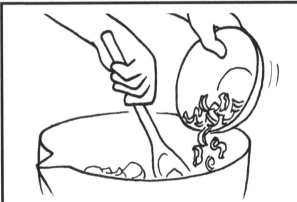

10. Add bacon and onion and mix.

11. Add mayonnaise and mix.

12. Add chives and pepper, mix and serve.

Teaching Healthy Cooking and Nutrition, Book 3

Potato Salad

Ingredients:
300g potatoes
3 rashers streaky bacon
1 onion
4 tbsp mayonnaise
Pinch of pepper
Fresh chives

Equipment:
Saucepan
Turner
Potato peeler   Mixing bowl
Colander   Scissors
Sharp knife   Mixing spoon
Tablespoon   Frying pan
Chopping board   Scales

Instructions:

1.   Put water in a saucepan and put on hob.

2.   Peel potatoes.

3.   Cut potatoes and put in boiling water.

4.   Cut bacon into small pieces.

5.   Peel and chop onion.

6.   Cut chives with scissors.

7.   Fry bacon in frying pan. Remove when cooked.

8.   Fry onions in frying pan.

9.   Drain potatoes when ready and put in bowl.

10.   Add bacon and onion and mix.

11.   Add mayonnaise and mix.

12.   Add chives and pepper, mix and serve.

Cheese Straws

How to Use a Palette Knife

Palette knives are used to loosen and remove cookies and other delicate foods from a baking tray or dish. They are easy to use because they are flexible and long. They are often used to slide cookies safely on and off baking trays without breaking them. Slide the blade flat-edged under the food and move back and forth gently. This action will loosen any food from the baking tray without it breaking.

Cheddar is from the Cheddaring Process

Theory

Cheddar is now made all over the world, although it originated in the Somerset village of Cheddar. Cheddaring refers to a unique process in the making of cheddar cheese, whereby, after heating, the curd (solid) is cut into cubes to drain the whey (liquid). The cubes are then stacked and turned. It is the cheddaring process that makes cheddar cheese.

Hot-tap Water Temperatures

Health & Safety

Hot-tap Water Must Be Below 49°Celsius.

The water coming out of the hot-water tap must be below 49°C. If it is any hotter, it will burn and scald you before you can remove your hand. Young children and old people, in particular, are in danger of getting burnt by hot water. On most mixer taps, there is in fact a thermostatic mixing valve installed. This is to make sure that the water coming out of the tap never exceeds 49°C.

Any burns should be treated immediately by cooling the skin with cold water, and seeking medical help.

Recipe

Cheese Straws

Ingredients:

50g wholemeal flour   50g plain flour   50g margarine
50g cheese   1 egg   Pinch of dry mustard
Pinch of salt and pepper

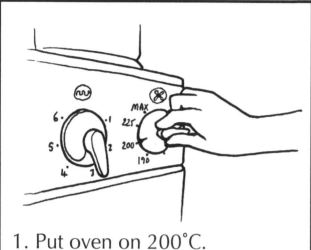

1. Put oven on 200°C.

2. Sieve flours, salt, pepper and dry mustard into bowl.

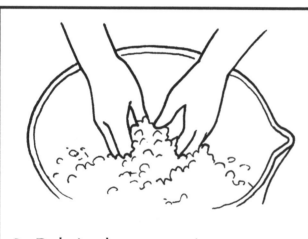

3. Rub in the margarine.

4. Grate the cheese and add to bowl. Mix.

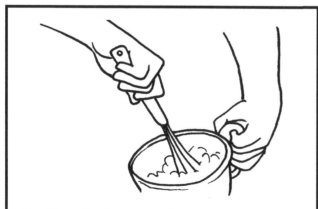

5. Crack the egg into a cup. Whisk.

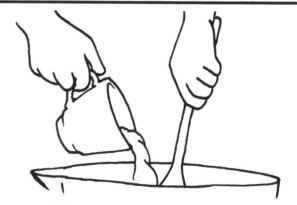

6. Add egg to mixture and mix to form dough.

Cheese Straws (cont.)

Recipe

Equipment:

Mixing bowl	Flour dredger	Mixing spoon	Rolling pin
Scales	Knife	Sieve	Palette knife
Grater	Baking tray	Cup	Whisk/fork

7. Sprinkle work surface with flour.

8. Roll dough out into a rectangle.

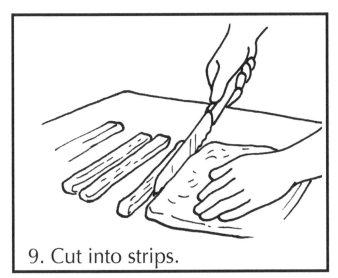

9. Cut into strips.

10. Grease tray.

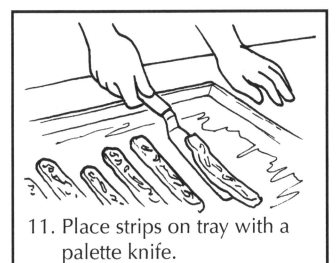

11. Place strips on tray with a palette knife.

12. Bake for 10–15 minutes.

Recipe

Cheese Straws

Ingredients:
50g wholemeal flour
50g plain flour
50g margarine
50g cheese
1 egg
Pinch of dry mustard
Pinch of salt and pepper

Equipment:
Mixing bowl
Flour dredger
Mixing spoon   Palette knife
Rolling pin   Grater
Scales   Baking tray
Knife   Cup
Sieve   Whisk/fork

Instructions:
1.   Put oven on 200°C.

2.   Sieve flours, salt, pepper and dry mustard into bowl.

3.   Rub in the margarine.

4.   Grate the cheese and add to bowl. Mix.

5.   Crack the egg into a cup. Whisk.

6.   Add egg to mixture and mix to form dough.

7.   Sprinkle work surface with flour.

8.   Roll dough out into a rectangle.

9.   Cut into strips.

10.   Grease tray.

11.   Place strips on tray with a palette knife.

12.   Bake for 10–15 minutes.

Naan Bread

Skill

How to Follow a Recipe

It is important to follow a recipe. Once you know a lot about food, you can begin to be more experimental, but it is best to start by following the recipe from beginning to end. Get into some sort of routine. It is important to get all the equipment and ingredients ready first. Perhaps tick off the instructions as you go. Always remember to double-check that you have completed an instruction before you go on to the next.

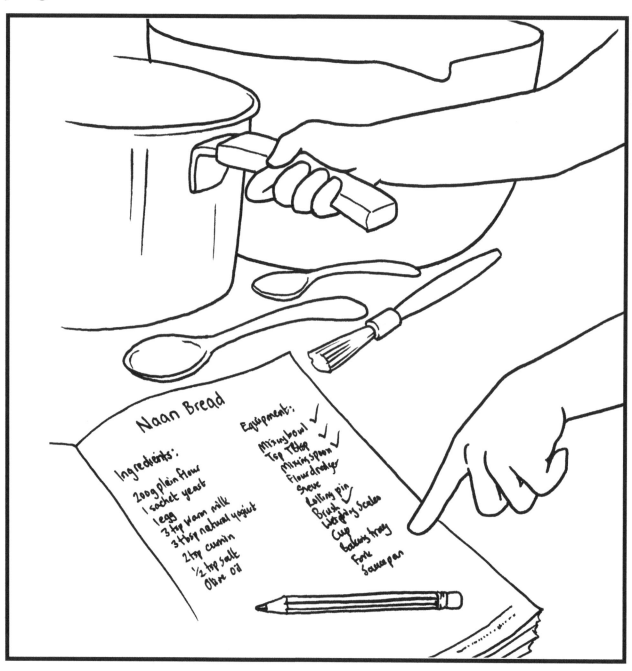

Naan is an Asian type of bread

Naan is a type of flatbread that you might get with an Indian meal. It has a soft texture and is often used to scoop up other food, especially curries. Naan bread is traditionally cooked in a Tandoor. A Tandoor is a clay oven with a charcoal fire inside. If you do not have a Tandoor oven, you can grill the naan instead.

Water and Electricity Don't Mix

Avoid touching anything electrical with wet hands.

Never let anything electrical come into contact with anything wet. This is because water is an excellent conductor of electricity. In other words: electricity can travel through water and give you an electric shock – and these can sometimes kill people. In a kitchen or cooking area, where there are electrical appliances, such as ovens, blenders, toasters and kettles, you have to be extra careful. Never touch electrical appliances with wet hands and never use electrical appliances next to or near taps.

Naan Bread

Ingredients:

200g plain flour	1 sachet yeast	3 tbsp milk
2 tsp cumin	3 tbsp natural yogurt	1 egg
1/2 tsp salt	Olive oil	

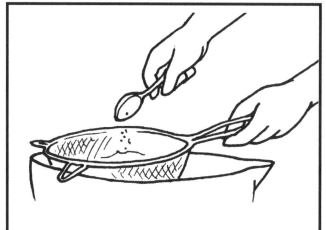

1. Sieve flour and salt into a bowl.

2. Add the yeast and mix.

3. Crack an egg into a cup and whisk.

4. Put milk, yogurt and egg into a saucepan.

5. Heat to lukewarm.

6. Add milk mixture to bowl and mix to form dough.

Naan Bread (cont.)

Equipment:

Mixing bowl	Cup	Mixing spoon	Flour dredger
Rolling pin	Sieve	Scales	Whisk/fork
Teaspoon	Brush	Baking tray	Saucepan	Tablespoon

Recipe

7. Sprinkle work surface with flour.

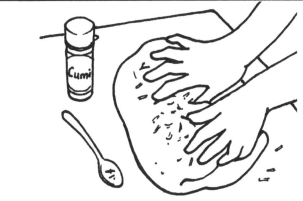

8. Knead cumin seeds into the dough for 5 minutes.

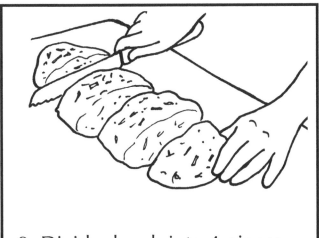

9. Divide dough into 4 pieces.

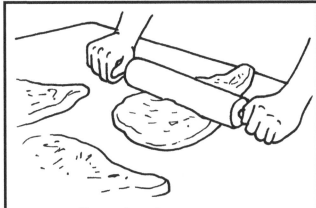

10. Roll each piece out to a teardrop shape.

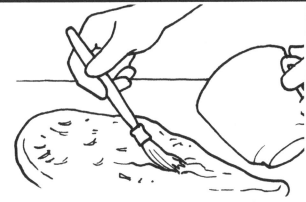

11. Brush both sides with olive oil and put on baking tray.

12. Grill each side on high for 2 minutes or until risen and golden.

© Sandra Mulvany and Brilliant Publications

This page may be photocopied by the purchasing institution only.

Teaching Healthy Cooking and Nutrition, Book 3

www.brilliantpublications.co.uk   **35**

Naan Bread

Recipe

Ingredients:
200g plain flour
1 sachet yeast
3 tbsp milk
2 tsp cumin
3 tbsp natural yogurt
1 egg
1/2 tsp salt
Olive oil

Equipment:
Mixing bowl
Cup
Mixing spoon
Flour dredger   Teaspoon
Rolling pin   Tablespoon
Sieve   Brush
Scales   Baking tray
Whisk/fork   Saucepan

Instructions:

1. Sieve the flour and salt into a bowl.

2. Add the yeast and mix.

3. Crack an egg into a cup and whisk.

4. Put milk, yogurt and egg into a saucepan.

5. Heat to lukewarm.

6. Add milk mixture to bowl and mix to form dough.

7. Sprinkle work surface with flour.

8. Knead cumin seeds into the dough for 5 minutes.

9. Divide dough into 4 peices.

10. Roll each piece out to a teardrop shape.

11. Brush both sides with olive oil and put on baking tray.

12. Grill each side on high for 2 minutes or until risen and golden.

Cheese and Courgette Muffins

How to Use Measuring Spoons

When you have to measure ingredients with spoons, you can use specially made measuring spoons. These come in many sizes, including teaspoon size and table-spoon size. Measuring spoons are more accurate than normal spoons and are easier to use. However, you may not always have measuring spoons to hand, so practise using both measuring spoons and normal spoons. Use a knife to scrape the top of the spoon so that you have a level spoonful.

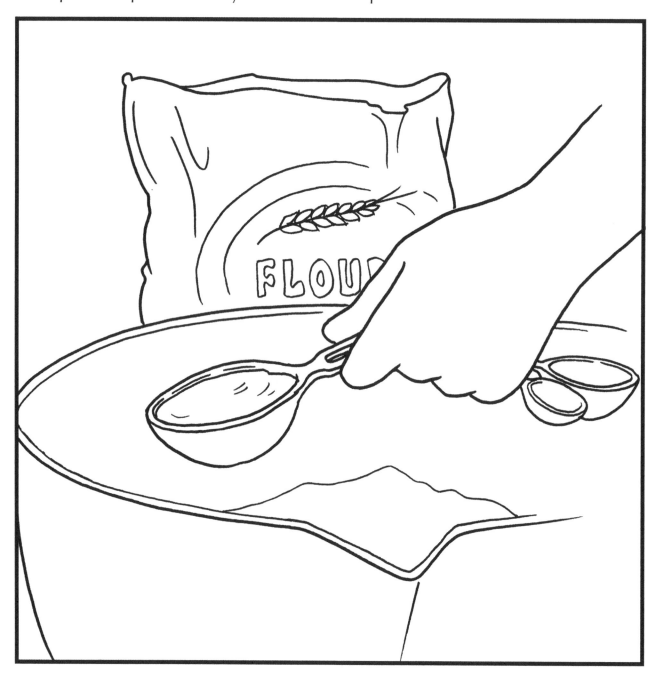

Eggs as a Raising Agent

Theory

Eggs, when beaten, help to make food rise.

Eggs have the ability to trap air. When you whisk eggs, bubbles of air will get trapped in the liquid. Although this is most obvious when whisking egg white, it is also the case to a lesser extent with whole eggs. Therefore, when you mix your whisked egg into the muffin mixture, the trapped air bubbles in it will help the muffins rise. Other well-known recipes using this method of whisking eggs to make them rise are soufflés and meringues.

Fridge Temperatures

Health & Safety

The temperature inside a fridge should be 5°C or just below (ideally between 3.3°C and 1.7°C). The purpose of refrigeration is to slow down the growth of bacteria. If the temperature is any higher, the food will spoil too quickly, but remember, keeping food cold, only delays this chemical reaction. Over time milk will go sour, cheese will grow mould, vegetables will wilt and meat will start to decompose. By putting food in the fridge, we allow ourselves a little extra time to store these foods before they spoil. However, if the temperature goes below 0°C, freezing will occur and some foods will spoil.

Care must always be taken to ensure that all fresh meats are kept at just below 5°C as harmful bacteria can multiply rapidly if the temperature gets any higher.

Recipe

Cheese and Courgette Muffins

Ingredients: 100g self-raising flour   1 tsp baking powder
1 tbsp milk   25g Parmesan   1 small courgette
1 egg   1 tbsp olive oil   50ml natural yogurt   Pinch salt & pepper

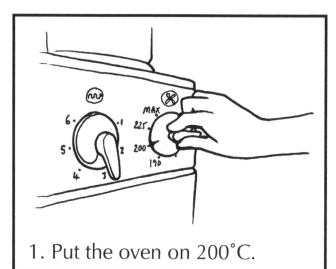

1. Put the oven on 200°C.

2. Weigh the flour and put in a bowl.

3. Add salt and pepper.

4. Add baking powder and Parmesan and mix.

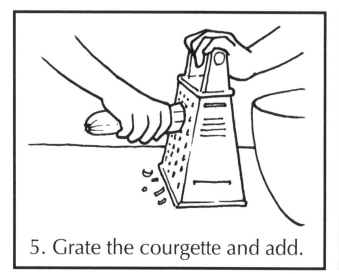

5. Grate the courgette and add.

6. Put milk in a separate bowl.

Cheese and Courgette Muffins (cont.)

Recipe

Equipment:

	2 mixing bowls	Mixing spoon	Scales
Teaspoon	Tablespoon	Grater	Cup
Whisk/fork	6 muffin cases	Baking tray	

7. Add oil and yogurt.

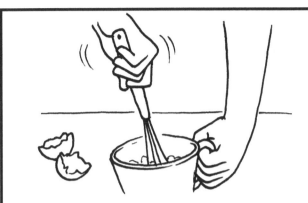

8. Crack the egg into a cup and whisk.

9. Add to milk mixture and mix.

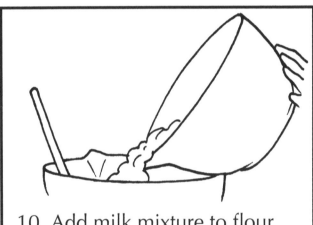

10. Add milk mixture to flour and mix.

11. Spoon mixture into muffin cases. Place on baking tray.

12. Bake for 10–15 minutes.

Cheese and Courgette Muffins

Ingredients:
100g self-raising flour
1 tsp baking powder
1 tbsp milk
25g Parmesan
1 small courgette
1 egg
1 tbsp olive oil
50ml natural yogurt
Pinch salt & pepper

Equipment:
2 mixing bowls
Mixing spoon
Scales
Teaspoon
Tablespoon
Grater
Cup
Whisk/fork
6 muffin cases
Baking tray

Instructions:

1. Put the oven on 200°C.

2. Weigh the flour and put in a bowl.

3. Add salt and pepper.

4. Add baking powder and Parmesan and mix.

5. Grate the courgette and add.

6. Put milk in a separate bowl.

7. Add oil and yogurt.

8. Crack the egg into a cup and whisk.

9. Add to milk mixture and mix.

10. Add milk mixture to flour and mix.

11. Spoon mixture into muffin cases. Place on baking tray.

12. Bake for 10–15 minutes.

Leek and Potato Soup

How to Use a Hand Blender

Be careful when you use a hand blender. It can easily splash hot liquids on you. If the liquid is in a saucepan, put the saucepan on a heat-resistant chopping board. Then put your hand blender into the liquid and start blending. Always keep the blender under the surface of the liquid to avoid any splashes. Move the blender around gently under the surface until you have the consistency that you want. Make sure that the saucepan isn't going to move when you blend. Also, beware the sharp blades of any blender – these can cut you.

What is a Leek?

Theory

Leeks are related to onions. They have long been used in European and Mediterranean cooking. Nowadays, they are available in supermarkets year-round, and so are easy to get. In Wales, leeks symbolize an important battle that the Welsh won against the Saxons in the 7th century AD. In that battle, the Welsh warriors wore leeks in their hats so that they could tell themselves apart from the Saxons.

Water and Elecricity Don't Mix

Health & Safety

Never touch electrical appliances with wet hands.

Never touch anything electrical if you have wet hands. This is because it can give you an electrical shock. Obviously, you need to be aware of this risk when you blend liquids with an electrical blender. Never plug in or unplug the blender with wet hands. Make sure the blender has been correctly assembled and is safe before using it.

Leek and Potato Soup

Ingredients:

1 leek   1 potato   1 onion   25g margarine   Water
1 vegetable stock cube   100ml single cream

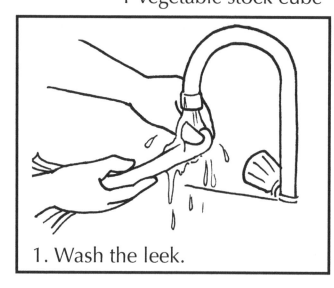

1. Wash the leek.

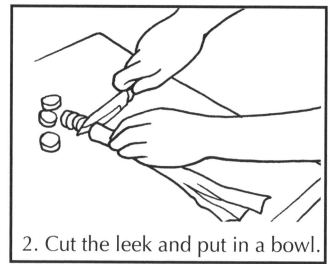

2. Cut the leek and put in a bowl.

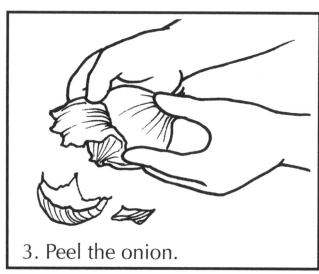

3. Peel the onion.

4. Cut the onion and add to bowl.

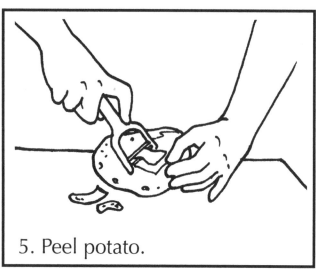

5. Peel potato.

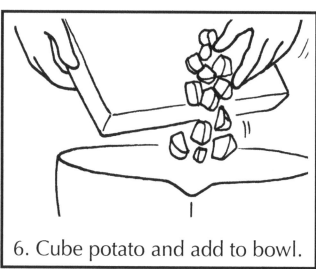

6. Cube potato and add to bowl.

Leek and Potato Soup (cont.)

Equipment:

Chopping board   Sharp knife   Peeler   Saucepan

Mixing bowl   Mixing spoon   Hand blender

7. Put a saucepan on the hob.

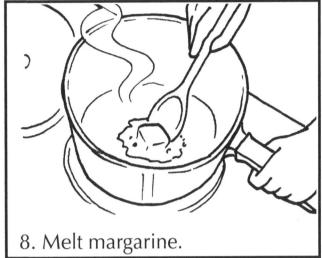

8. Melt margarine.

9. Add leek, onion and potato and fry lightly.

10. Add water to cover. Add stock cube and simmer for 10 minutes.

11. Put saucepan on a chopping board. Blend.

12. Add cream last, mix and serve.

Skill

Leek and Potato Soup

Ingredients:
1 leek
1 potato
1 onion
25g margarine
Water
1 vegetable stock cube
100ml single cream

Equipment:
Chopping board
Sharp knife
Peeler
Saucepan
Mixing bowl
Mixing spoon
Hand blender

Instructions:

1. Wash the leek.

2. Cut the leek and put in a bowl.

3. Peel the onion.

4. Chop the onion and add to bowl.

5. Peel potato.

6. Cube potato and add to bowl.

7. Put a saucepan on the hob.

8.   Melt margarine.

9. Add leek, onion and potato and fry lightly.

10. Add water to cover. Add stock cube and simmer for 10 minutes.

11. Put saucepan on a chopping board. Blend.

12. Add cream last, mix and serve.

Beef Burgers

© Sandra Mulvany and Brilliant Publications

This page may be photocopied by the purchasing institution only.

Teaching Healthy Cooking and Nutrition, Book 3

www.brilliantpublications.co.uk **49**

How to Shape a Burger

Use both hands to shape a burger. Pick up a small handful of the mixture and shape it as you would shape a snowball. Then pressing it flat, place it on a chopping board and make sure that the burger has the same height all over. It is important that the mixture is pressed together firmly, so that it does not fall apart during frying. Remember to wash your hands after you have touched the raw meat, and also to wash the chopping board and utensils well to avoid cross-contamination.

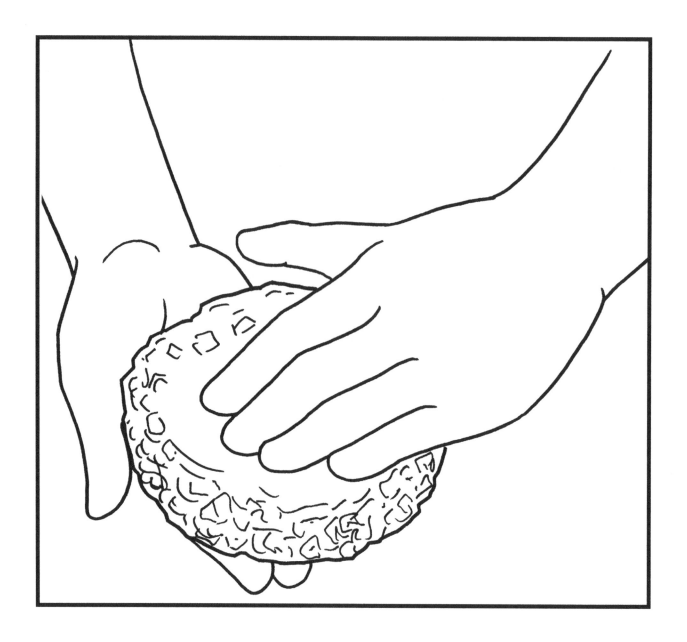

Where Does Meat Come from?

There are many different types of "meat": beef, pork, lamb, poultry and fish. Meat comes from the flesh of animals such as cows, pigs and sheep. Most meat we eat comes from animals specifically bred for this purpose on farms. It is important to make sure that the animal you eat had a good life before it was slaughtered – and that the slaughter was carried out in a humane way. Animals should be allowed as much freedom as possible to live out their lives in a reasonably natural way – as opposed to being kept in cramped, crowded conditions.

The origins of the meat must be always be shown on the labelling.

Oil Pan Fires

How to put out an oil fire in a frying pan.

When oil in a frying pan gets too hot, it will catch fire. The only thing to do is for an adult to drape a fire blanket or wet towel over the pan to cut off the oxygen, thereby putting out the fire. NEVER pour water over burning oil, as it will actually make the fire "explode". This is because water is denser than oil and so sinks to the bottom of the pan. The water will instantly vaporize because of the heat and release the air upwards along with the burning oil, causing an "explosion". Standard fire extinguishers do NOT work either, as the oil is, in fact, too hot. These types of fires result in over 50 deaths per year in the UK.

Recipe

Beef Burgers

Ingredients: 225g lean minced beef   25g breadcrumbs
1 small egg   1 tsp ketchup   1 tsp mustard
Pinch of pepper   Oil   (Tomato, lettuce, bread rolls)

1. Put the meat in a bowl.

2. Add the breadcrumbs.

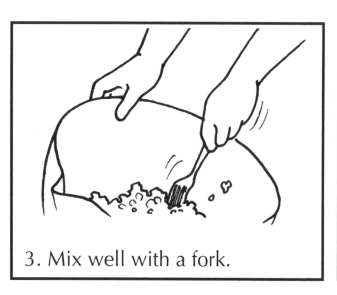

3. Mix well with a fork.

4. Crack the egg into a cup and whisk.

5. Put egg in another bowl.

6. Add ketchup and mustard and mix.

Beef Burgers (cont.)

Recipe

Equipment:
2 bowls   Scales   Fork   Cup   Teaspoon
Frying pan   Chopping board   Turner   Whisk/fork

7. Add pepper and mix.

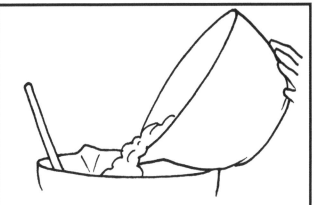

8. Add egg mixture to meat mixture and mix well.

9. Shape to form burgers.

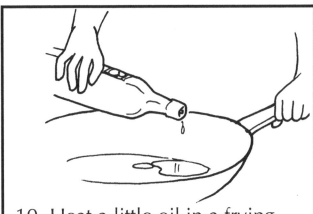

10. Heat a little oil in a frying pan.

11. Fry the burgers on both sides.

12. Serve in a roll with lettuce and tomato.

Recipe

Beef Burgers

Ingredients:
225g lean minced beef
25g breadcrumbs
1 small egg
1 tsp ketchup
1 tsp mustard
Pinch of pepper
Oil
(Tomato, lettuce, bread rolls)

Equipment:
2 bowls
Scales
Fork
Cup
Teaspoon
Frying pan
Chopping board
Turner
Whisk/fork

Instructions:

1.	Put the meat in a bowl.

2.	Add the breadcrumbs.

3.	Mix well with a fork.

4.	Crack the egg into a cup and whisk.

5.	Put egg into another bowl.

6.	Add ketchup and mustard and mix.

7.	Add pepper and mix.

8.	Add egg mixture to meat mixture and mix well.

9.	Shape to form burgers.

10.	Heat a little oil in a frying pan.

11.	Fry the burgers on both sides.

12.	Serve in a roll with lettuce and tomato.

Apple Muffins

© Sandra Mulvany and Brilliant Publications

This page may be photocopied by the purchasing institution only.

Teaching Healthy Cooking and Nutrition, Book 3

www.brilliantpublications.co.uk   **55**

How to Spoon Mixture into Cases

Use two teaspoons when you spoon mixture into cake cases. Scoop up some of the mixture with one of the teaspoons and then holding the spoons over a muffin case, push the mixture off of the spoon with the back of the second teaspoon. Always use the back of the teaspoon to spoon out with, otherwise the mixture will just get stuck. If the mixture hangs onto the second teaspoon, use the first to scrape this off. Make sure the mixture does not drip onto the bun tin, as this will only burn.

Sieving Flour Helps Cakes Rise

Theory

When you sieve flour, you not only get rid of the lumps, you also add air to the flour. The finer the flour is sieved, the more air you add. It is a bit like "fluffing up" a pillow. The more air there is in the flour and cake mixture, the more the cake will rise.

Using Knives Safely

Health & Safety

Always make sure you cut directly downwards.

When you go to cut with a sharp knife, always make sure that the blade is pointing directly downwards. It mustn't point diagonally at all. This is because of the risk of cutting into your fingers or losing control of the knife. Before you start cutting, make sure you know that the knife will go into the chopping board only. Also remember that the blade may look the same on the top and on the bottom, but one side is very sharp.

Recipe

Apple Muffins

Ingredients:
125g self-raising flour   1 egg   1 tsp margarine
1 green apple   75ml milk   25g caster sugar

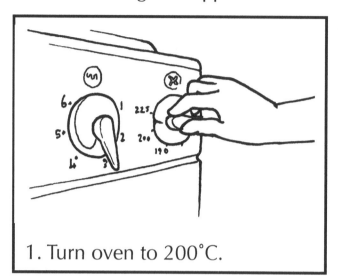

1. Turn oven to 200°C.

2. Sieve the flour into a bowl.

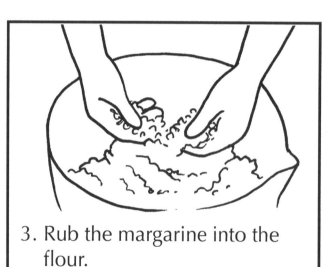

3. Rub the margarine into the flour.

4. Add the sugar and mix.

5. Measure the milk in a measuring jug.

6. Crack the egg into a cup and whisk.

Apple Muffins (cont.)

Equipment: Mixing bowl   Sieve   Chopping Board
Sharp knife   Muffin cases   Bun tin   2 Teaspoons
Whisk/fork   Measuring jug   Cup   Scales

7. Add the egg to the milk and mix.

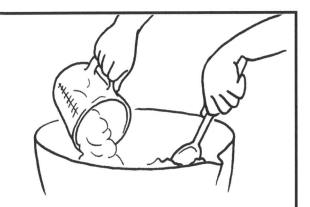

8. Add the milk mixture to the flour gradually and mix.

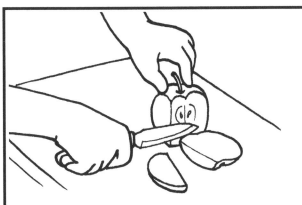

9. Cut around the core of the apple.

10. Cut apple into small pieces, add to mixture and mix.

11. Spoon mixture into cases.

12. Bake for 10–15 minutes.

Teaching Healthy Cooking and Nutrition, Book 3

Recipe

Apple Muffins

Ingredients:
125g self-raising flour
1 egg
1 tsp margarine
1 green apple
75ml milk
25g caster sugar

Equipment:
Mixing bowl
Sieve
Chopping board
Sharp knife
Muffin cases
Bun tin
2 Teaspoons
Whisk/fork
Measuring jug
Cup
Scales

Instructions:

1. Put oven on 200°C.

2. Sieve the flour into a bowl.

3. Rub the margarine into the flour.

4. Add the sugar and mix.

5. Measure the milk in a measuring jug.

6. Crack the egg into a cup and whisk.

7. Add the egg to the milk and mix.

8. Add the milk mixture to the flour gradually and mix.

9. Cut around the core of the apple.

10. Cut apple into small pieces, add to mixture and mix.

11. Spoon mixture into cases.

12. Bake for 10–15 minutes.

Tuna in Salad

Skill

How to Toss a Salad

To "toss" a salad simply means to "mix" a salad. You can easily toss a salad with two tablespoons. You simply put the spoons into the salad and turn the salad over and over again until you are sure that all the ingredients are well mixed.

What is an Oily Fish?

An "oily fish" is a type of fish which has oil in the fillet and around the gut. This is different from "white fish" which only has oil in the liver. Oily fish are a good source of vitamin A and vitamin D and are also very rich in omega 3. For this reason, oily fish are healthier than white fish. Typical types of oily fish are: trout, salmon, mackerel, herring, sardines and fresh tuna. Typical types of white fish are: cod, plaice and haddock. Unfortunately, due to the canning process of tuna, most omega 3 is actually lost in tinned tuna. Therefore, although tinned tuna is healthy, it is considered a white fish as far as omega 3 content is concerned. Luckily, this does not apply to other tinned fish.

Putting on a Plaster

If someone gets a small cut, you should rinse it under the cold tap. Then you gently dry the cut with a sterile tissue and put a plaster on it. Try to place the middle of the plaster on the cut and remove the two flaps without actually touching the plaster. This will minimize the risk of any infection. The purpose of the plaster is precisely to protect the cut from water, dirt and germs that may cause infection.

Tuna in Salad

Ingredients: 1 tin of tuna   6 cherry tomatoes
Lettuce leaf   50g pasta   1 onion   Water
6 pitted black olives   Italian dressing

1. Boil the pasta.

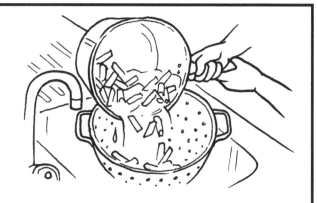

2. Drain the pasta when ready and put into bowl.

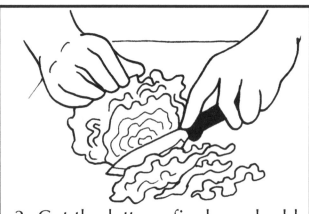

3. Cut the lettuce finely and add to bowl.

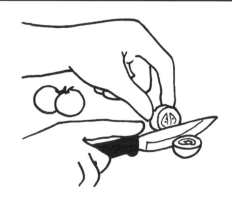

4. Halve the cherry tomatoes and add to bowl.

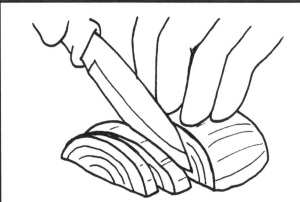

5. Slice the onion finely and add to bowl.

6. Halve the olives and add to bowl.

Tuna in Salad (cont.)

Equipment:

Saucepan	Colander	Chopping board	Sharp knife
2 mixing bowls	Tin opener	Sieve	Fork	2 tablespoons	Scales

Recipe

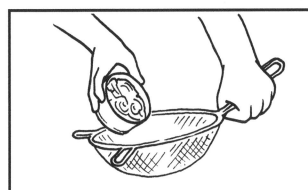

7. Open the tin of tuna and pour into a sieve over the sink.

8. Let the tuna drain.

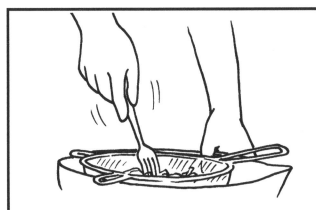

9. Break the tuna into flakes with a fork.

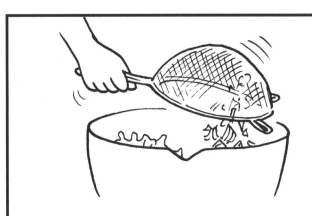

10. Add tuna to salad bowl and toss.

11. Pour over a little dressing.

12. Toss the salad again.

Recipe

Tuna in Salad

Ingredients:
1 tin of tuna
Leaf lettuce
50g pasta
6 cherry tomatoes
1 onion
6 pitted black olives
Italian dressing
Water

Equipment:
Saucepan
Colander
Chopping board
Sharp knife
2 mixing bowls
Tin opener
Sieve
Fork
2 tablespoons
Scales

Instructions:

1. Boil the pasta.

2. Drain the pasta when ready and put into bowl.

3. Cut the lettuce finely and add to bowl.

4. Halve the cherry tomatoes and add to bowl.

5. Slice the onion finely and add to bowl.

6. Halve the olives and add to bowl.

7. Open the tin of tuna and pour into a sieve over the sink.

8. Let the tuna drain.

9. Break the tuna into flakes with a fork.

10. Add tuna to salad bowl and toss.

11. Pour over a little dressing.

12. Toss the salad again.

Yogurt and Herb Rolls

© Sandra Mulvany and Brilliant Publications

This page may be photocopied by the purchasing institution only.

Teaching Healthy Cooking and Nutrition, Book 3

www.brilliantpublications.co.uk   **67**

How to Check Bread Rolls

To check whether your bread rolls are ready, you simply take one out of the oven and tap it on the bottom (be careful not to get burnt). If it sounds hollow, it is done. If all the rolls are the same size, they should all be ready.

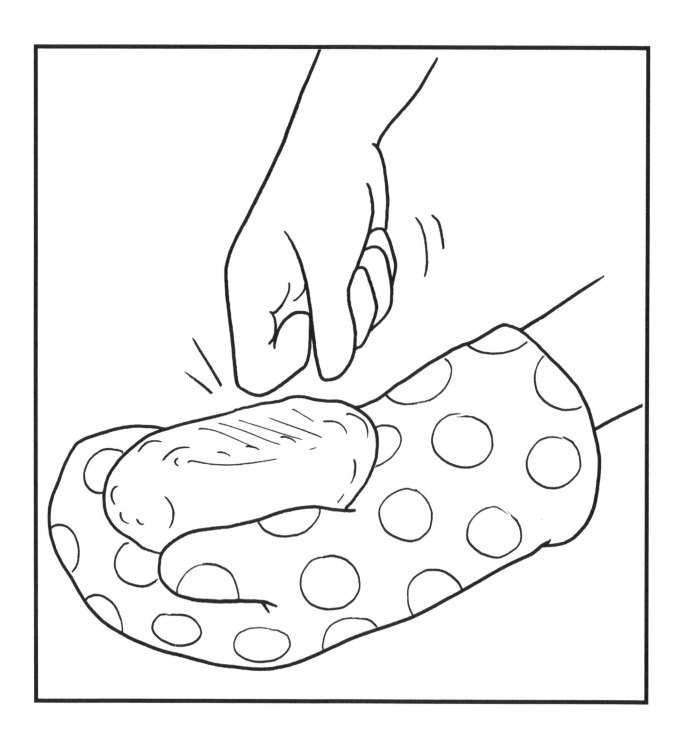

About Yogurt

Not only is yogurt a wonderful quick, easy snack that is available all-year-round, but researchers have found evidence that milk and yogurt may actually add years to your life (as in countries where fermented dairy products are part of the staple diet).

Yogurt is a fermented dairy product made from adding bacterial cultures to milk, which causes the transformation of the milk's sugar (lactose) into lactic acid. This process gives yogurt its refreshingly tart flavour and unique pudding-like texture, a quality that is reflected in its original Turkish name, Yoghurmak, which means "to thicken".

Burns

What to do if you burn yourself (minor burns).

If you burn yourself on an oven door or hob, put the burnt area under cold, running tap water straight away. Do this for at least 5 minutes or until the pain stops. Cooling the burn reduces the swelling by conducting the heat away from the skin.

Yogurt and Herb Rolls

Ingredients: 100g plain flour   2 tbsp margarine
1 tsp baking powder   1 egg   ½ tsp bicarbonate of soda
30g sugar   1 tsp mixed herbs   150ml natural yogurt

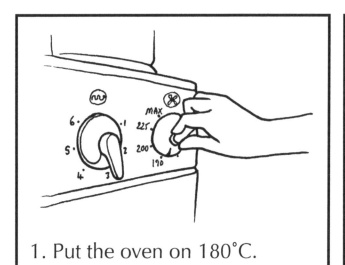

1. Put the oven on 180°C.

2. Sieve the flour into a bowl. Rub in margarine.

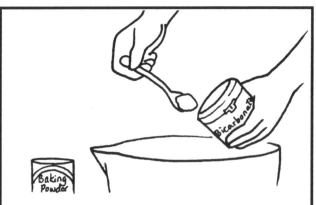

3. Add the baking powder and bicarbonate of soda.

4. Put yogurt in another bowl.

5. Crack an egg into a cup and whisk.

6. Add egg and sugar to yogurt.

Yogurt and Herb Rolls (cont.)

Equipment: 2 mixing bowls   Cup   Mixing spoon
Whisk/fork   Measuring jug   Sieve   Teaspoon
Tablespoon   Baking tray   Scales   Flour dredger

Recipe

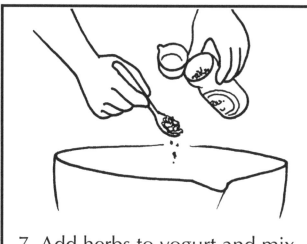

7. Add herbs to yogurt and mix.

8. Add yogurt mixture to flour mixture and mix to form dough.

9. Sprinkle hands with flour and shape into rolls.

10. Put on a greased baking tray.

11. Bake in the oven for 10–15 minutes.

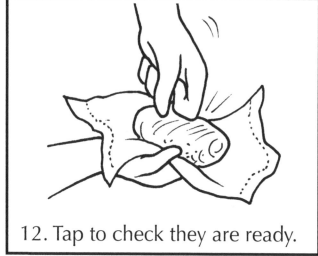

12. Tap to check they are ready.

Yogurt and Herb Rolls

Recipe

Ingredients:
100g plain flour
2 tbsp margarine
1 tsp baking powder
1 egg
½ tsp bicarbonate of soda
30g sugar
150ml natural yogurt
1 tsp mixed herbs

Equipment:
2 mixing bowls
Cup
Mixing spoon
Whisk/fork
Measuring jug
Sieve   Baking tray
Teaspoon   Scales
Tablespoon   Flour dredger

Instructions:

1.   Put the oven on 180°C.

2.   Sieve the flour into a bowl. Rub in margarine.

3.   Add the baking powder and bicarbonate of soda.

4.   Put yogurt in another bowl.

5.   Crack an egg into a cup and whisk.

6.   Add egg and sugar to yogurt.

7.   Add herbs to yogurt and mix.

8.   Add yogurt mixture to flour mixture and mix to form a dough.

9.   Sprinkle hands with flour and shape into rolls.

10. Put on a greased baking tray.

11. Bake in the oven for 10–15 minutes.

12. Tap to check they are ready.

TIP
If the dough is too moist, add a little more flour from the flour dredger.

Vegetable Stir Fry

Skill

How to Use a Frying Pan

To stir fry vegetables, put them in a frying pan with a small amount of oil. Fry the vegetables quickly over a very high heat. This means that you need to have everything ready and be very careful. Hold the handle of the frying pan whilst you move the vegetables around with a turner. If it starts to smoke, remove the frying pan from the hob.

Saturated Fats and Cholesterol

Saturated fat is bad for your heart.

Too much saturated fat can lead to heart attacks and strokes. Heart attacks and strokes happen when arteries (the tubes that carry blood from your heart to the rest of your body) get clotted up and stop the blood from reaching the heart or brain. One of the reasons that arteries clot up is cholesterol. Your body produces enough cholesterol, so you do not need the cholesterol found in saturated fat. The "extra" cholesterol contained in saturated fat will just get carried out into your arteries and clot them up. Saturated fat and cholesterol are found in butter, full-fat dairy products, eggs, the fat in meat and coconut oil. This doesn't mean you have to stop eating these foods altogether – these foods have other nutrient values. It just means that you should not over-indulge yourself on these foods.

Hot Oil can Catch Fire

Be careful when you stir fry, because hot oil can actually catch fire. This is, of course, a problem, since stir frying is done over high heat. The sign to look out for is when the oil begins to smoke. This will mean that the oil is close to catching fire. The smoke point varies for different oils, so unless you know the temperature of your oil's smoke point, you have to look out for the smoke. If you see it, remove the frying pan from the heat and allow it to cool down. Oils with a high smoke point are good for stir frying; these include: rapeseed oil (230°C), almond oil (225°C), olive oil (210°C) and grapeseed oil (200°C).

Recipe

Vegetable Stir Fry

Ingredients: 1 small courgette 1 red pepper   4 baby corn
4 mushrooms   4 mangetout pods 1 celery stick   1 carrot
1 tbsp oil   ½ red onion   Soy sauce   (Serve with noodles or rice)

1. Wash the vegetables.

2. Cut the pepper and put in a bowl.

3. Chop the onion and celery and put them into the bowl.

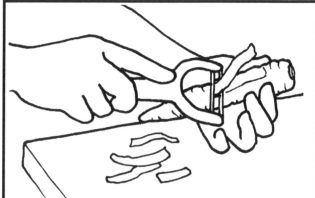

4. Peel and cut the carrot finely and add to the bowl.

5. Cut the courgette and put into a different bowl.

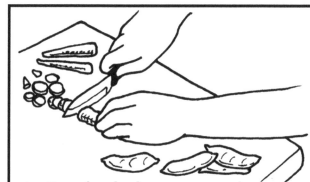

6. Cut the baby corn and mangetout and put them with the courgette.

Vegetable Stir Fry (cont.)

Equipment:

Chopping board   Sharp knife   2 bowls
Frying pan   Turner

7. Cut the mushrooms and leave them on chopping board.

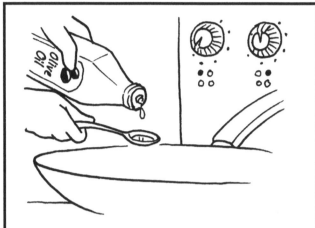

8. Heat oil in a frying pan.

9. Fry the pepper mixture first.

10. Add courgette mixture and then the mushrooms.

11. Add soy sauce and continue to fry until ready.

12. Serve with noodles or rice.

Teaching Healthy Cooking and Nutrition, Book 3

Recipe

Vegetable Stir Fry

Ingredients:
1 small courgette
1 red pepper
4 baby corn
4 mushrooms
4 mangetout pods
1 celery stick
1 carrot   ½ red onion
1 tbsp oil   Soy sauce
(Serve with noodles or rice)

Equipment:
Chopping board
Sharp knife
2 bowls
Frying pan
Turner

Instructions:

1.   Wash the vegetables.

2.   Cut the pepper and put in a bowl.

3.   Chop the onion and celery and put them in the bowl.

4.   Peel and cut the carrot finely and add to the bowl.

5.   Cut the courgette and put into a different bowl.

6.   Cut the baby corn and mangetout and put them with the courgette.

7.   Cut the mushrooms and leave them on chopping board.

8.   Heat oil in a frying pan.

9.   Fry the pepper mixture first.

10.   Add courgette mixture and then the mushrooms.

11.   Add soy sauce and continue to fry until ready.

12.   Serve with noodles or rice.

> **TIP**
> Add soya sauce to taste. About 2–3 tbsp should be about right.

Mashed Potatoes

How to Mash Potatoes

For best results, use a potato masher to mash boiled potatoes. The more you mash the potatoes, the smoother the mash will be. You can also add some butter, milk and/or cheese during the mashing process. This will change the texture and taste. You can even add herbs (such as chives) or a little nutmeg to the mash, if you like.

What is Calcium?

Children need calcium to grow.

Children are growing and developing all the time. Calcium is an essential mineral needed for their growing bones and their growing teeth. Dairy products (such as milk, cheese and yogurt) contain calcium, so they are particularly important in the diets of growing children. Calcium is of course also very important for adults, too, to help make sure that their teeth and bones stay healthy and strong.

Hazards in the Kitchen

Never leave sharp knives in water.

When you wash up, never leave a sharp knife in the water. You may forget it is there, and accidentally cut yourself. Alternatively, someone else may come along and put their hand into the water and cut themselves. When you wash a sharp knife, hold the handle and wash the blade carefully, then remove it and get someone to dry it carefully straight away – and then have it put away safely.

Mashed Potatoes

Ingredients: 350g potatoes   2 tbsp milk
2 tbsp chives   50g peas   50g Cheddar cheese
Water   Salt and pepper (optional)

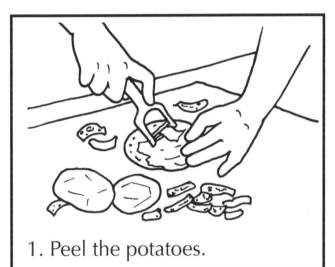

1. Peel the potatoes.

2. Chop the potatoes into cubes.

3. Put the potatoes in water in a saucepan.

4. Boil the potatoes until tender.

5. Cook the peas according to instructions on the packet.

6. Cut the chives.

Mashed Potatoes (cont.)

Equipment:

Peeler   Colander   Sharp knife   Chopping board   Masher

Sieve   Saucepan   Teaspoon   Mixing spoons   Tablespoon   Grater

7. Grate the cheese.

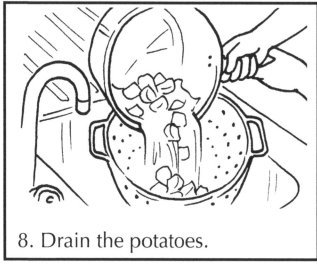

8. Drain the potatoes.

9. Mash the potatoes.

10. Add in the milk.

11. Mix in the cheese, chives and peas.

12. Season to taste and serve hot.

Teaching Healthy Cooking and Nutrition, Book 3

Mashed Potatoes

Ingredients:
350g potatoes
2 tbsp milk
2 tsp chives
50g peas
50g cheddar cheese
Water
Salt and pepper (optional)

Equipment:
Peeler
Colander
Sharp knife
Masher   Teaspoon
Sieve   Mixing spoon
Saucepan   Tablespoon
Chopping board Grater

Instructions:

1.   Peel the potatoes.

2.   Chop the potatoes into cubes.

3.   Put the potatoes in water in a saucepan.

4.   Boil the potatoes until tender.

5.   Cook the peas according to the instructions on the packet.

6.   Cut the chives.

7.   Grate the cheese.

8.   Drain the potatoes.

9.   Mash the potatoes.

10.   Add in the milk.

11.   Mix in the cheese, chives and peas.

12.   Season to taste and serve hot.

What Can You Remember? (1)

Take this quiz after Lesson 6.

1. How do you rub in?

    With your fingertips   With your palms   With an eraser

2. What happens to vitamin C in water?

    It puts on a life vest   It dissolves   It swims

3. What can happen if you use a wet knife?

    It can dissolve   It can slip   It can cut water

4. What is the hottest temperature hot tap water should be?

    49 °C   79 °C   99 °C

5. If the water is any hotter, what can it do?

    Melt the taps   Be used in chillies   Burn people

6. What happens if you mix electricity and water?

    You get an electric shock   You get drunk   You get tired

7. What can eggs trap?

    Air   Rabbits   Moles

8. What temperature should a fridge be?

    Below 0 °C   Below 5 °C   Below 10 °C

9. Which is the leek most like?

    Onion   Apple   Cucumber

10. What is one danger of using a hand blender?

    It can run off   It can hit you   It can splash hot liquid

Name _____ Date _____ Score _____

What Can You Remember? (2)

Take this quiz after Lesson 12.

1. Why should you always wash your chopping board, knife and hands straight-away after working with raw meat?

    To avoid doing cross country   To avoid cross-contamination   To avoid getting cross

2. How would you put out a fire caused by hot cooking oil?

    Use a fire blanket   Use water   Use more oil

3. Where should the sharp blade of a knife be pointing when you cut?

    Diagonally   Straight down   Up

4. Which food is the best source of protein?

    Apples   Tomatoes   Eggs

5. Which vitamin do eggs NOT contain?

    Vitamin A   Vitamin B   Vitamin C

6. What should yogurt contain?

    Bacteria   Salt   Ham

7. If you tap the bottom of a bun when it is ready, how does it sound?

    Full   Half empty   Hollow

8. Which type of fat is bad for you?

    Saturated fat   Saturn fat   Satisfied fat

9. How do you know when a cooking oil is close to catching fire?

    It starts to sing   It calls the fire brigade   It begins to smoke

10. What do children need calcium for?

    Fat bellies   Teeth and bones   Skin

Name _____ Date _____ Score _____

Certificate of Achievement

Teaching Healthy Cooking and Nutrition, Book 3

Name

Is Able to

Rub in

Peel a potato

Use a palette knife

Follow a recipe

Use measuring spoons

Use a hand blender

Shape a burger

Spoon into cases

Toss a salad

Check buns

Use a frying pan

Mash potatoes

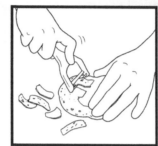

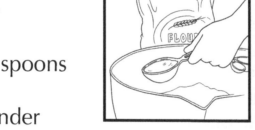

Allergy/lifestyle/religious considerations

The chart below lists possible substitutions that can be made (where possible) for children with common allergies/intolerances and/or lifestyle/religious considerations. It is not exhaustive and it is important to check with parents prior to doing any cooking activities.

Recipe	Possible substitutions
Cheesy Biscuits	This recipe is not suitable for children with gluten/wheat and/or egg allergies. (Alternative gluten free/egg free recipes can be found on the Internet.) Lactose free hard cheese and margarine may be used for children who are lactose intolerant.
Potato Salad	The bacon may be omitted for children who don't eat pork due to religious/lifestyle considerations. It is possible to buy egg-free mayonnaise for children with egg allergies.
Cheese Straws	This recipe is not suitable for children with gluten/wheat and/or egg allergies. (Alternative gluten free/egg free recipes can be found on the Internet.) Lactose free hard cheese and margarine may be used for children who are lactose intolerant.
Naan Bread	This recipe is not suitable for children with gluten/wheat and/or egg allergies. (Alternative gluten free/egg free recipes can be found on the Internet.) It is possible to buy lactose-free yogurt and milk (eg rice or oat milk) in large supermarkets for children with a lactose intolerance.
Cheese and Courgette Muffins	For children with gluten/flour allergies, gluten free flour and baking powder may be substituted. The dough will be stickier than when made with normal flour. This recipe is not suitable for children with egg allergies. It is possible to buy lactose-free yogurt in large supermarkets for children with a lactose intolerance. Some children may be unable to eat aged cheeses, such as Parmesan, either because they are lactose intolerant, or as they are sensitive to the histamines that are found naturally in these cheeses. Check with parents first.

Allergy/lifestyle/religious considerations (cont.)

Recipe	Possible substitutions
Leek and Potato Soup	It is possible to buy dairy free cream for children who are lactose intolerant. Use lactose free margarine as well. Check whether the stock cube contains gluten if you have a child with a gluten allergy.
Beef Burgers	This recipe is not suitable for vegetarians. Use gluten free bread crumbs (and gluten free bread rolls) for children with gluten/wheat allergies. You can omit the egg for children with egg allergies, but the burgers will not stick together as well.
Apple Muffins	This recipe is not suitable for children with gluten/wheat and/or egg allergies. (Alternative gluten free/egg free recipes can be found on the Internet.) Lactose free milk and margarine may be used for children who are lactose intolerant.
Tuna in Salad	Some vegetarians will eat fish, but others won't. Check with the parents. Use gluten free pasta for children with gluten/free allergies.
Yogurt and Herb Rolls	This recipe is not suitable for children with gluten/wheat and/or egg allergies. (Alternative gluten free/egg free recipes can be found on the Internet.) Lactose free yogurt and margarine may be used for children who are lactose intolerant.
Vegetable Stir Fry	If anyone has a soy allergy, then the soy sauce should be omitted.
Mashed Potatoes	If a child is lactose intolerant, substitute the milk with some of the water that the potatoes were cooked in. It is possible to buy lactose free hard cheese in most large supermarkets.